Grill

Grill

Delicious recipes for your electric grill

Linda Doeser

p

This is a Parragon Publishing Book
First published in 2005

Parragon Publishing
Queen Street House
4 Queen Street
Bath
BA1 1HE, UK

Copyright © Parragon 2005

All rights reserved. No part of this publication may be reproduced, stored in a retrieval
system, or transmitted, in any form or by any means, electronic, mechanical, photocopying,
recording, or otherwise, without the prior permission of the copyright holder.

ISBN: 1-40545-118-1

Printed in China

Author: Linda Doeser
Editor: Fiona Biggs
Designed by Fiona Roberts
Photography: Karen Thomas
Home Economist: Valerie Berry

Notes for the Reader

This book uses both imperial and US cup measurements. All spoon measurements are
level; teaspoons are assumed to be 5 ml and tablespoons are assumed to be 15 ml.
Unless otherwise stated, milk is assumed to be full fat, individual vegetables such as
potatoes are medium, and pepper is freshly ground black pepper. Recipes using raw or
very lightly cooked eggs should be avoided by infants, the elderly, pregnant women,
convalescents and anyone suffering from an illness. Pregnant and breastfeeding women
are advised to avoid eating peanuts and peanut products. The times given are an
approximate guide only. Preparation times differ according to the techniques used by
different people and the cooking times may also vary from those given. Optional
ingredients, variations, or serving suggestions have not been included in the calculations.

Contents

INTRODUCTION   PAGE 6

SNACKS AND LIGHT BITES   PAGE 12

MEAT AND POULTRY   PAGE 24

FISH AND SHELLFISH   PAGE 48

VEGETARIAN   PAGE 70

SWEET TREATS   PAGE 86

INDEX   PAGE 96

INTRODUCTION

The grill is one of the most recent electrical kitchen appliances to hit the stores and has quickly become extremely popular. This may be because we have become increasingly health-conscious and keen to reduce the quantity of fat in our diet—certainly this is one major advantage of cooking this way.

It may equally be that its rapid cooking times are immensely appealing in our rushed twenty-first century lifestyle. It may also be because it's very easy to use and more reliable than many conventional broilers. The risk of spitting fat burning the cook or catching fire is virtually non-existent. The electric grill reduces the problem of lingering cooking smells and is easy to clean. They are available in such a wide range of sizes that there is a model to suit everyone.

The electric grill is rather like a pair of griddle pans joined with a hinge in an elaborate—and usually much bigger—version of a sandwich toaster. There are two ridged plates, which are set at an angle to let fat drain off into a drip tray. Having two plates allows the food to be cooked on both sides simultaneously, reducing the cooking time considerably. The grill plates have a nonstick coating, making them easy to clean. In some models, these are removable and dishwasher safe. In others, they are fixed and can be wiped clean with a damp cloth or sponge. The drip tray may be either a simple container that you position slightly under the front of the electric grill in the center or an integral part of the appliance that slides out from the front. Both are easy to empty and wash and are usually dishwasher safe. The hinge is articulated so it can be

adjusted to accommodate different thicknesses of food while keeping the grilling plates parallel. A thermostatically controlled light indicates when it has been fully preheated.

Some models offer a variety of extra features, such as a variable temperature control, a digital or analog timer and even a roll warmer for burgers and hot dogs. Sizes vary from an appliance that will cook two chicken breast portions or burgers up to one that can cook as many as ten at the same time with several intermediate sizes along the way. Thus there is an electric grill that will suit virtually all needs from the single person to the extended family.

Choosing an electric grill

The size of the grill is one of the first considerations. It's a waste of electricity and space to buy a huge grill if you rarely cook for more than two or three people, while on the other hand, it's self-defeating to have one that means you're forever cooking in batches. Taking average chicken breast portions or fish steaks (about 6 oz) as a reasonable guide, the following size grilling plates are suitable for cooking the number of servings listed on the right.

The size of the grill will also affect the price and the amount of storage room you will need to find. Another factor to consider, which also affects the price, is the inclusion of extra features. A timer that beeps is a useful reminder, but is not absolutely essential and you should not use this as an excuse to leave the electric grill unattended when in use.

Grill plate size chart	
37–39 sq inches	**2 servings**
62 sq inches	**4 servings**
78 sq inches	**5 servings**
85–100 sq inches	**6 servings**
124 sq inches	**8 servings**
132 sq inches	**10 servings**

Variable temperature settings—sometimes as many as five—allow for greater flexibility and are probably worth considering if you are a very keen or experimental cook. However, they are not essential. A roll warmer is likely to be a must-have if your home is the haunt of a bunch of adolescents, most of whom seem to have hollow legs that can be satisfied only with a frequent intake of burgers. Otherwise, it's probably superfluous to most people's needs.

The recipes in this book have been tested on a basic family-size electric grill with an indicator light and a single temperature setting but no "extras." They are therefore suitable for use on all makes and models. If you have a variable temperature control, check the manufacturer's handbook for guidance on temperature and timing.

Using the electric grill

As with all electrical appliances, you should read the manufacturer's handbook carefully before using the grill. Although they all work in much the same way, it is important to understand exactly how to use your particular model.

The electric grill should always be used indoors—it is not a substitute for a barbecue. Place it on a level, heat-resistant surface not too close to the sink and out of the reach of children. It is also a sensible precaution to keep it clear of drapes, racks of dish towels, or anything that might catch fire. Before you switch it on, make sure that the grill is stable and that the cable is not hanging over the edge of the counter or trailing across the lid, which gets very hot. The drip tray should be empty and in position.

Brush the grilling plates evenly with a little oil—sunflower, peanut, corn, or olive oil, for example—close the lid and switch on to preheat. Usually the light comes on during preheating and goes out when it is ready for use. Preheating takes about 5 minutes, but will vary with different temperatures. Wearing an oven mitt, open the lid and place the food in a single layer on the bottom plate using a plastic or wooden spatula or tongs. Do not touch the plate with your fingers. Close the lid, checking that the top and bottom grilling plates are more or less parallel. Set the grill timer or an ordinary kitchen timer or check the clock. Do not leave the electric grill unattended while it is switched on.

When the time is up, put on an oven mitt and open the grill. Cooking times on pages 10–11 and in the recipes are approximate because ingredients vary in thickness and density, so you need to check if the food is cooked through. It is best to remove the food to a plate using tongs or a spatula before checking. If the food is not cooked through, return it to the grill for 1–2 minutes more, then check again.

Chicken, other poultry, and pork should be cooked until the juices run clear. The easiest way to check is to pierce the thickest part with the point of a knife. If there are any traces of pink or red, return the food to the grill for a little longer. Meat products, such as burgers and sausages, should also be checked in the same way. Fish is cooked when the flesh is opaque and flakes easily with a fork. Tuna is an occasional exception as it is often served still red in the middle, but this is a matter of taste. Similarly, beef may be served still red in the middle and lamb when it is still pink in the middle. Check by making a small incision to see if it is done to your liking.

Cooking times

The following cooking times apply to some common fresh ingredients at room temperature. If you are cooking ready-prepared food, read the pack instructions and remember that the food will be cooked on both sides simultaneously.

Hints and tips

◎ Do not switch on the grill to preheat if you have more than about 5 minutes' preparation still to do.

◎ Prepare ingredients for garnishing, decorating, or serving pockets, before you start cooking.

◎ Trim off excess fat from meat before cooking.

◎ Try to make sure that ingredients such as fish steaks or lamb chops are about the same thickness to insure even cooking. Slice or dice vegetables and fruit into even pieces.

◎ Thinner foods cook more quickly. As a general rule, do not try use the grill for anything that is thicker than about 1 inch. That is why the list of cooking times includes chicken breast portions and thighs, but not drumsticks. Boneless meat and poultry can be gently pounded flat. Place delicate meat, such as chicken breast portions, between 2 sheets of plastic wrap and pound with a rolling pin or the flat side of a meat bat until thin and even. Remove and discard the plastic wrap before adding the meat to the grill.

◎ As the grill cooks so quickly, always check food at the end of the specified cooking time. It's simple to pop it back in for an extra minute, but there's nothing you can do if it's overcooked. Remember to remove it from the grill first.

◎ Always wear an oven mitt when opening or closing the grill lid once it has been switched on.

Cooking times chart

Meat and poultry	Minutes
Beef burger 4 oz	7–8
Beef burger 8 oz	8–9
Chicken breast portion	5–7
Chicken thighs	5–7
Fillet steak	5–7
Gammon steak	5–6
Kabobs*	7–8
Lamb chops	4–6
Pork chops	5–6

	Minutes
Pork tenderloin	4–6
Round steak	7–8
Sausages**	5–8
Sirloin steak	7–9
T-bone steak	8–9
Turkey burger 4 oz	5
Turkey scallops	3–4
Turkey steaks	5–6
Beef, lamb, pork, or chicken	
**Beef or pork*	

Fish and shellfish	Minutes
Cod fillet*	3–5
Cod steak*	6–8
Kabobs (shellfish)	3–6
Kabobs (fish/mixed fish and shellfish)	4–6
Mackerel fillet**	4–5
Salmon fillet	3–4
Salmon steak	6–8
Sea scallops	4–6
Shrimp	1–2
Sole fillet***	3–4

◎ If cooking from frozen, allow an additional 3–6 minutes for meat and poultry, 3–4 minutes for fish, and 1–2 minutes for shellfish.

◎ If you want to use the grill for toasted sandwiches, make them with the buttered side of the bread outermost. Do not make them more than ¾ inch thick and place them on the grilling plate with a plastic spatula. Most sandwiches take about 6 minutes, plain cheese takes about 3 minutes.

◎ Always use a nonmetallic spatula or kitchen tongs to add food to the grill and to remove it. The grilling plates become very hot and are not suitable places for fingers. Don't use metal tools which can damage the nonstick coating.

◎ Make sure that the drip tray is empty and in position.

◎ Brush the grilling plates with oil before preheating. You can also use melted butter, but low-fat spreads are not suitable as they have a low burning point.

◎ Make sure that the grill and its cable are out of the reach of children and never leave a switched-on grill unattended.

◎ Drain ingredients that have been marinating before adding them to the grill. A lot of oily marinade sloshing about could catch fire.

◎ Don't forget to turn the grill off when you've finished.

Care of the electric grill

When you've finished cooking, switch off and unplug the grill, then let cool completely. Empty the drip tray. Wipe out the drip tray with paper towels and put it back in position. When the grill is cold remove the grilling plates and wash in the dishwasher or warm soapy water. If the plates are fixed, wipe them with a damp cloth or sponge, then dry with paper towels. Rub stains or burned-on marinade with a paper towel dipped in vegetable oil. Do not use scouring pads or abrasive cleaners. Wash the drip tray in the dishwasher, if approved by the manufacturer, or in warm soapy water. Rinse and dry before storing. Never immerse the grill in water.

	Minutes
Squid	3–4
Tuna steak****	6–9

* Also other white fish, such as halibut, porgy, red snapper

** Also other oily fish fillets, such as herring

*** Also other flat fish, such as flounder, dab

**** Also other oily fish, such as swordfish

Vegetables	Minutes
Asparagus (whole)	3–4
Bell pepper (halved)	8–9
Bell pepper (sliced)	6–8
Carrot (sliced)	5–7
Eggplant (sliced)	8–9
Garlic (sliced)	5–6
Leek (baby whole)	3–4
Mushroom (sliced)	3–5
Onion (sliced)	5–6
Onion (wedges)	6–7
Potato (sliced)	7–9
Tomato (sliced)	3–5
Zucchini (sliced)	6–8

Fruit	Minutes
Apple (sliced)	6–8
Banana (sliced)	3–4
Kabobs	3–5
Mango (sliced)	3–5
Peach (sliced)*	3–5
Peach halved*	4–6
Pear (sliced)	5–8
Pineapple (sliced)	4–7

* Also nectarines and apricots

1

CHAPTER 1: SNACKS AND LIGHT BITES

SPICY SHRIMP

Jumbo shrimp always look so tempting, and when they are served with this colorful dip they are simply irresistible.

 Serves 4

Preparation time: 15 minutes

Cooking time: 1 hour/2 minutes' grilling

Ingredients

24 raw jumbo shrimp, thawed if frozen

1 bay leaf

2 tbsp lime juice

1 tsp hot paprika

2 shallots, coarsely chopped

1 garlic clove, coarsely chopped

1 tbsp light soy sauce

1 tbsp peanuts

1 tbsp dry unsweetened coconut

1/2 red bell pepper, seeded and chopped

7 oz canned tomatoes

sunflower oil, for brushing

salt and pepper

lime wedges, to garnish

1 Pull the heads off the shrimp and peel off the shells. Place the head, shells, and bay leaf in a pan and add enough cold water to cover. Bring to a boil, then lower the heat, and simmer for 30 minutes.

2 Meanwhile, using a sharp knife, cut along the back of each shrimp. Remove the dark vein with the point of the knife. Place the shrimp in a nonmetallic dish and sprinkle with the lime juice and paprika. Season with salt and pepper and toss well to coat. Cover with plastic wrap and let marinate in the refrigerator.

3 Put the shallots, garlic, soy sauce, peanuts, coconut, and bell pepper in a food processor. Drain the tomatoes, reserving 5 tablespoons of the can juice. Add the tomatoes and the reserved can juice to the food processor. Process until smooth. Scrape the mixture into a pan.

4 When the shellfish stock is ready, strain it into a pitcher, pour it into the pan, and bring the mixture to a boil, stirring occasionally. Lower the heat and simmer for 25–30 minutes until thickened.

5 Brush the electric grill with oil and preheat. Remove the shrimp from the refrigerator and thread them loosely onto skewers to make handling them easier. When the grill is hot, add the shrimp, and cook for 2 minutes, or until they have changed color and are cooked through.

6 Transfer the shrimp to a serving dish—with or without the skewers—and garnish with lime wedges. Pour the dipping sauce into a bowl and serve with the shrimp.

SURPRISE SIZZLES

These are closely related to a barbecue recipe called pigs in blankets.

Sausages are filled with melting cheese and wrapped in slices of bacon.

🍽 Serves 4

🥄 Preparation time: 5 minutes

🧤 Cooking time: 8–13 minutes

Ingredients

sunflower oil, for brushing

1 lb pork sausage links

4 oz Cheddar cheese, sliced

8 bacon slices

4 tsp Dijon mustard

1 Brush the electric grill with oil and preheat. When the grill is hot, add the sausages and cook for 5 minutes if they are thin and 8 minutes if they are thick. They should be evenly golden brown.

2 Remove them from the grill and, using a sharp knife, spilt them lengthwise without cutting all the way through. Fill them with the cheese slices, then press them back together. If necessary, cut off the bacon rinds with kitchen scissors. Spread the mustard over the bacon and wrap the slices around the sausages. Secure the ends with wooden toothpicks.

3 Return the sausages to the grill and cook for 3–5 minutes more until the cheese has melted and the bacon is crisp. Serve immediately.

Cook's tip
You can use any good-quality pork sausages for this recipe. Sausages that are flavored with sage or other herbs work particularly well.

Variation
Those who prefer a hotter flavor can substitute a stronger mustard for the Dijon. Milder mustards, such as German or American, can also be used.

Hot Dogs

*As well as being one of the world's favorite snacks,
this must also be one of the quickest and easiest.*

⦿ Serves 4
🥄 Preparation time: 10 minutes
🧤 Cooking time: 8 minutes

Ingredients

sunflower oil, for brushing

6 tbsp tomato ketchup

2 tbsp French mustard

2 scallions, finely chopped

1 fresh green chili, seeded and
   finely chopped

4 hot dog rolls

1 onion, thinly sliced into rings

4 large frankfurter sausages

1 Brush the electric grill with oil and preheat. Meanwhile, combine the tomato ketchup, mustard, scallions, and chili in a bowl. Split the hot dog rolls.

2 When the grill is hot, add the onion and cook for 5 minutes, or until softened and beginning to color. Remove the onion rings, add the frankfurters to the grill, and cook for 3 minutes. Using tongs, place the frankfurters in the rolls, top with the onion rings and sauce, and serve.

Cook's tip
For plain hot dogs, omit the mustard, scallions, and chili and simply serve the frankfurters in the split rolls with onions and ketchup.

TOMATO TOASTS

These make great snacks or appetizers and taste best when you use sun-ripened tomatoes, which are full of sweetness and flavor.

Serves 4

Preparation time: 10 minutes

Cooking time: 2 minutes

Ingredients

olive oil, for brushing and drizzling

4 thick slices sourdough or whole-wheat bread

6 plum tomatoes, thickly sliced

sherry vinegar or red wine vinegar, for sprinkling

1 oz freshly shaved Parmesan cheese

salt and pepper

fresh basil leaves, to garnish

1 Brush the electric grill with oil and preheat. Toast the bread on both sides in a toaster or under a broiler. Place the toast slices on warm serving plates.

2 When the grill is hot, add the tomato slices and cook for 2 minutes. Arrange the tomato slices on top of the toasted bread and drizzle with olive oil. Sprinkle with a little vinegar and season with salt and pepper.

3 Sprinkle the Parmesan shavings over the top of the toasts, garnish with fresh basil leaves and serve immediately.

Cook's tip
Sprinkle rather than drizzle the vinegar over the toasts. Here it is being used as a light seasoning, not a dressing.

Variation
For extra flavor grill 4 thinly sliced garlic cloves at the same time as the tomatoes.

MIXED VEGETABLE BRUSCHETTA

*Garlic-flavored toasts piled high with Mediterranean vegetables are
wonderful served as a colorful appetizer or a tasty lunchtime snack.*

Serves 4

Preparation time: 15 minutes

Cooking time: 9 minutes

Ingredients

olive oil, for brushing and drizzling

1 red bell pepper, halved and seeded

1 orange bell pepper, halved and seeded

4 thick slices baguette or ciabatta

1 red onion, sliced

1 fennel bulb, sliced

2 zucchini, sliced diagonally

2 garlic cloves, halved

1 tomato, halved

salt and pepper

fresh sage leaves, to garnish

1 Brush the electric grill with oil and preheat. Cut each bell pepper half lengthwise into 4 strips. Toast the
bread slices on both sides in a toaster or under a broiler.

2 When the grill is hot add the bell peppers and fennel and cook for 4 minutes, then add the onion and
zucchini, and cook for 5 minutes more until all the vegetables are tender but still with a slight "bite."
If necessary, cook the vegetables in 2 batches, as they should be placed on the grill in a single layer.

3 Meanwhile, rub the garlic halves over the toasts, then rub them with the tomato halves. Place on warm
plates. Pile the grilled vegetables on top of the toasts, drizzle with olive oil, and season with salt and
pepper. Garnish with sage leaves and serve warm.

Cook's tip
*The exact timing depends on how thinly you slice the
vegetables and on how soft you want them to be. Remove
the ones that are done at the end of the cooking time and
cook the remainder for 1–2 minutes more.*

Variation
*You could also include eggplant slices. There is no need to
salt them first. Place them on the electric grill with the bell
peppers and fennel to cook for a total of 8–9 minutes.*

CHEESE QUESADILLAS

These crisp Mexican snacks are usually deep-fried, but cooking them on the electric grill works just as well and is healthier.

|◯| Serves 6

Preparation time: 10 minutes

Cooking time: 4–6 minutes

Ingredients
corn oil, for brushing

8 oz queso anejo or Cheddar
  cheese, grated

3 jalapeño chilies, seeded and chopped

12 ready-made tortillas

salt

1 red onion, thinly sliced, to garnish

1 Brush the electric grill with oil and preheat. Combine the grated cheese and chilies in a bowl and season with a little salt.

2 Hold a tortilla flat in one hand and sprinkle a tablespoonful of the cheese mixture along the center. Fold the tortilla over and press the edges together to seal. Fill the other tortillas in the same way.

3 When the grill is hot, add the filled tortillas, in batches, and cook for 2–3 minutes. Garnish with onion slices and serve immediately.

Cook's tip
Queso anejo, which means aged cheese, is a traditional hard cheese from Mexico. Although originally made from goat milk, nowadays it is more often made from cow's milk. The sharp cheese is ideal for cooking and has a texture like that of Parmesan.

Variation
You can make quesadillas with all kinds of fillings, including sliced chorizo, refried beans, lightly fried sliced onion, and shredded cooked chicken. Chilies, however, are non-negotiable.

CHAPTER 2: MEAT AND POULTRY

STEAK BÉARNAISE

Cooking the perfect steak is not as easy as people sometimes think, but using the electric grill reduces the risk of overcooking or uneven cooking.

○ Serves 4

Preparation time: 10 minutes

Cooking time: 25 minutes/6–8 minutes' grilling

Ingredients

6 tbsp white wine vinegar

2 bay leaves

10 black peppercorns

2 shallots, finely chopped

3 fresh tarragon sprigs

olive oil, for brushing

4 egg yolks

1 cup sweet butter, cut
   into small pieces

2 tbsp chopped fresh tarragon

4 sirloin steaks, trimmed of fat

salt and pepper

fresh watercress sprigs or arugula, to garnish

1 Put the vinegar, bay leaves, peppercorns, shallots, and tarragon sprigs into a pan and bring to a boil. Lower the heat and simmer until reduced to 2 tablespoons. Remove the pan from the heat, strain the vinegar into a bowl, and let cool.

2 Brush the electric grill with oil and preheat. Beat the egg yolks with salt and pepper in a heatproof bowl. Set the bowl over a pan of barely simmering water and beat in the cooled vinegar. Gradually beat in the butter, 1 piece at a time. Beat in the chopped tarragon and remove the pan from the heat but leave the bowl set over it to keep the sauce warm. Cover the surface with dampened waxed paper to prevent a skin from forming.

3 When the grill is hot add the steak and cook for 6–8 minutes, depending on how well done you like your steak and how thick it is. (This will produce medium rare to medium.) Check the steak and continue cooking for 1–2 minutes if it is too rare.

4 Transfer the steaks to warm plates. Remove and discard the waxed paper from the sauce. Stir, then spoon a little over each steak. Garnish with watercress sprigs or arugula leaves and serve immediately.

Cook's tip

For best results the steaks should be of an even thickness of no more than 1 inch. If you like, pound them with a meat bat or rolling pin before cooking.

STEAK TERIYAKI

Marinating the steaks in this piquant sauce imbues them with a rich, slightly sweet flavor that is irresistible.

Serves 4

Preparation time: 10 minutes, plus 6 hours' marinating

Cooking time: 6–8 minutes

Ingredients

1 tbsp cornstarch

1/2 cup dark soy sauce

2 tbsp honey

2 tbsp rice vinegar

4 tbsp mirin

4 sirloin steaks, trimmed of fat

sunflower oil, for brushing

salad greens, to serve

1 Combine the cornstarch and soy sauce in a pitcher until smooth, then stir in the honey, vinegar, and mirin. Place the steaks in a shallow, nonmetallic dish and pour the marinade over them. Turn to coat, then cover with plastic and leave in the refrigerator to marinate for at least 6 hours.

2 Remove the steaks from the refrigerator and bring back to room temperature. Brush the electric grill with oil and preheat. Drain the steaks, reserving the marinade. Place the marinade in a small pan and bring to a boil.

3 Meanwhile, when the grill is hot add the steaks and cook for 6–8 minutes, depending on how well done you like your steak and how thick it is. (This will produce medium rare to medium.) Check the steak and continue cooking for 1–2 minutes if it is too rare.

4 Transfer the steaks to warm serving plates and spoon the hot sauce over them. Serve immediately with salad greens.

Cook's tip

Mirin is a sweet Japanese rice wine, available from some supermarkets and specialty stores. If you can't find it, use medium sherry instead, but not Chinese rice wine, which is much drier.

Variation

Substitute skinless boneless chicken breast portions for the steaks and grill them for 5–7 minutes. Check that they are cooked through by piercing with the point of a knife (remove them from the grill first). If the juices run clear, they are ready. If not, return them to the grill for 1–2 minutes.

HOMEMADE BURGERS

Much tastier than the ready-made variety—and a lot healthier too, especially if you grind lean steak yourself.

Serves 4
Preparation time: 10 minutes
Cooking time: 5–6 minutes

Ingredients
2 onions

1 lb 5 oz lean ground steak

5 tbsp fresh white bread crumbs

1 tsp chopped fresh thyme

1 egg, lightly beaten

sunflower oil, for brushing

salt and pepper

To serve
4 burger rolls

shredded lettuce

sliced tomatoes

mayonnaise

ketchup

1 Finely chop 1 onion and thinly slice the other. Put the steak, bread crumbs, chopped onion, and thyme into a bowl, season with salt and pepper, and mix well. Add the egg and mix with your hands until thoroughly combined. Divide the mixture into 4 portions and shape each into a patty no more than 1 inch thick. Set aside on a plate.

2 Brush the electric grill with oil and preheat. Halve the burger rolls and make a bed of shredded lettuce on each bottom half.

3 When the grill is hot add the sliced onion and burgers and cook, turning the burgers once, for 5–6 minutes. Check that the burgers are cooked through and that the juices run clear when pierced with the point of a knife (remove them from the grill first). If they're not done, return them to the grill for 1–2 minutes.

4 Place the burgers on the lettuce, top with the sliced onion and tomato slices and the other halves of the rolls. Serve immediately with mayonnaise and ketchup.

Cook's tip
For a healthier burger, use reduced-calorie mayonnaise or, better still, substitute mild mustard.

CHILIBURGERS

This popular variation of the familiar burger certainly adds spice to life. Serve in burger rolls with plenty of cooling salad ingredients to balance the heat.

Serves 6

Preparation time: 10 minutes

Cooking time: 5–6 minutes

Ingredients

7 oz canned kidney beans, drained
  and rinsed

1 lb lean ground steak

8 oz bulk pork sausage

1 garlic clove, finely chopped

1 onion, finely chopped

2 tsp chili powder

sunflower oil, for brushing

salt and pepper

1 Chop the kidney beans and place in a bowl with the steak, bulk sausage, garlic, onion, and chili powder. Season with salt and pepper and mix well until thoroughly combined.

2 Brush the electric grill with oil and preheat. Divide the mixture into 6 portions and shape into patties no more than 1 inch thick.

3 When the grill is hot add the burgers and cook, turning once, for 5–6 minutes. Check that the burgers are cooked and that the juices run clear when pierced with the point of a knife. If they're not done, return them to the grill for 1–2 minutes.

Cook's tip
These burgers are terrific served with guacamole or tomato relish.

Variation
If you prefer you can substitute 2–3 seeded and finely chopped fresh green chilies for the chili powder.

DRUNKEN LAMB

A very unusual marinade gives lamb chops an intriguing flavor
that is deliciously matched with shallot butter.

Serves 4

Preparation time: 15 minutes, plus 30 minutes' marinating

Cooking time: 5–7 minutes

Ingredients

4 lamb leg chops or 8 lamb loin chops

2 garlic cloves, finely chopped

3 tbsp dry gin

3 tbsp lime juice

3 tbsp olive oil, plus extra for brushing

3 tbsp Worcestershire sauce

generous $\frac{1}{2}$ cup finely chopped shallots

$\frac{2}{3}$ cup sweet butter, softened

salt and pepper

garlic mash, to serve (optional)

1 Place the chops in a single layer in a large, shallow, nonmetallic dish. Combine the garlic, gin, lime juice, olive oil, and Worcestershire sauce in a pitcher and season to taste with salt and pepper. Pour the mixture over the chops and turn them to coat. Cover with plastic wrap and set aside in a cool place to marinate for 30 minutes.

2 Blanch the shallots in boiling water for 2–3 minutes. Drain and pat dry with paper towels. Process in a blender or food processor to a purée. Add the butter, season with salt and pepper, and process until thoroughly combined. Scrape the flavored butter onto a piece of foil. Roll into a cylinder shape and chill until required.

3 Brush the electric grill with oil and preheat. Drain the chops and, when the grill is hot add them and cook for 5–7 minutes, depending on their thickness and how well done you like your lamb. They may be served slightly pink in the middle or well done. Loin chops will cook slightly more quickly than leg chops.

4 Unwrap the shallot butter and cut into slices. Transfer the chops to warm plates, top with 1–2 slices of the butter, and serve with garlic mash if you like.

Cook's tip
If you are planning to marinate the chops for longer than 30 minutes, then you can chill the butter in the refrigerator. Otherwise, place it in the freezer to make sure that it has set before serving.

Variation
This recipe also works well with pork chops, provided that they are not too thick. Cook on the electric grill for 5–6 minutes and check that the juices run clear by piercing with the point of a knife. If there are any traces of pink, return the chops to the grill for 1–2 minutes more.

Louisiana Lamb

Lamb chops are coated with a fabulous Cajun spice mix and served with a refreshing salsa.

Serves 4

Preparation time: 15 minutes, plus 6 hours' marinating and 1 hour's standing

Cooking time: 5–7 minutes

Ingredients

2 tbsp sunflower oil, plus extra for brushing

2 tsp ground coriander

2 tsp ground cumin

1 tsp mild paprika

1 tsp chili powder

1 tsp garlic powder

1/2 tsp ground turmeric

1/2 tsp ground cloves

1/2 tsp dried oregano

8 lamb loin chops or 4 lamb leg chops

Salsa

3 scallions, chopped

2 tomatoes, seeded and chopped

1 fresh Anaheim or mild serrano chili, seeded and chopped

1 tbsp lime juice

1 tbsp olive oil

1 tbsp chopped fresh cilantro

dash of Tabasco sauce

1 Combine the oil, coriander, cumin, paprika, chili powder, garlic powder, turmeric, cloves, and oregano in a large bowl. Add the lamb chops and mix well to coat. Cover with plastic wrap and marinate in the refrigerator for 6 hours or overnight.

2 Remove the lamb from the refrigerator and let return to room temperature. To make the salsa, combine all the ingredients in a bowl, cover with plastic wrap, and set aside in a cool place (but not in the refrigerator) for 1 hour for the flavors to mingle.

3 Brush the electric grill with oil and preheat. When the grill is hot add the chops and cook for 5–7 minutes, depending on their thickness and how well done you like your lamb. They may be served slightly pink in the middle or well done. Loin chops will cook slightly more quickly than leg chops.

4 Taste the salsa, adding lime juice or Tabasco sauce to taste. Serve the chops with the salsa on the side.

Cook's tip

If you like, you can tie a strip of scallion or a strip of banana leaf to the bone end of each chop—this will make the meat easier to handle when it is cooked.

Variation

You can use this spice mix on skinless boneless chicken breast portions or turkey steaks. Cook on the electric grill for 5–7 minutes and check that the meat is cooked through by piercing with the point of a knife. If the juices run clear, it is cooked; if not, return to the grill for 1–2 minutes.

CHILI PORK

Chops from today's hog breeds can often seem rather boring and lacking in flavor so they benefit from a tasty marinade.

Serves 6

Preparation time: 15 minutes, plus 2 hours' marinating

Cooking time: 5–6 minutes

Ingredients

½ onion, coarsely chopped

1 garlic clove,
coarsely chopped

4 tomatoes, peeled, seeded, and
coarsely chopped

1 green bell pepper, halved, seeded
and coarsely chopped

2 fresh green chilies, seeded
and coarsely chopped

4 tbsp medium-dry white wine

6 boneless pork chops or pork steaks

sunflower oil, for brushing

salt and pepper

fresh parsley sprigs, to garnish

1 Put the onion, garlic, tomatoes, bell pepper, chilies, and wine in a blender or food processor, season with salt and pepper, and process to a paste. Place the chops in a shallow, nonmetallic dish and spread the spice paste over them. Cover with plastic wrap and marinate in a cool place for 2 hours.

2 Brush the electric grill with oil and preheat. Remove the chops from the dish and scrape off the marinade into a small pan. Heat the marinade just to boiling point and keep warm.

3 When the grill is hot add the chops and cook for 5–6 minutes. Check that the juices run clear by piercing with the point of a knife. If there are any traces of pink, return the chops to the grill for 1–2 minutes.

4 Transfer the chops to warm plates and spoon the hot marinade over them. Garnish with parsley sprigs and serve immediately.

Cook's tip
If you marinate the chops in the refrigerator, remove them 30 minutes before you plan to cook to bring them back to room temperature.

Variation
This is also a good way to prepare skinless, boneless chicken breast portions which can also sometimes taste bland. Grill for 5–7 minutes and check that they are cooked through in the same way as for the pork chops.

HAM STEAKS WITH PARSLEY BUTTER

This is a perfect meal for a midweek supper as it is so simple and quick.
You can serve it simply with salad, or with French fries or mashed potatoes.

Serves 4
Preparation time: 10 minutes
Cooking time: 5–6 minutes

Ingredients

½ cup sweet butter, softened
2 tbsp chopped fresh parsley
dash of lemon juice
sunflower oil, for brushing
4 cured ham steaks
salt and pepper
fresh parsley sprigs, to garnish

1 Put the butter in a bowl and beat until creamy. Beat in the parsley and lemon juice and season with salt and pepper. Taste and add more lemon juice if necessary. Place in the refrigerator until required.

2 Brush the electric grill with oil and preheat. Meanwhile, using sharp kitchen scissors, trim any fat from the ham steaks and snip the edges to prevent them from curling up.

3 When the grill is hot add the ham steaks and cook for 5–6 minutes until tender. Transfer to warm serving plates and top with a spoonful of the flavored butter. Garnish with parsley sprigs and serve immediately.

Cook's tip
Cured ham steaks also go well with Shallot Butter
(see page 32).

Variation
Fish steaks can also be prepared like this and almost
as quickly. Grill for 6–9 minutes until the flesh is opaque
and flakes easily when tested with a fork.

LIME & LEMONGRASS CHICKEN

Coconut milk, ginger, lime juice, lemongrass, chilies, and fresh cilantro give chicken a wonderful Southeast Asian flavor.

Serves 4

Preparation time: 20 minutes, plus 2 hours' marinating

Cooking time: 5–7 minutes

Ingredients

4 skinless, boneless chicken breast portions

scant $\frac{1}{2}$ cup lime juice

$\frac{2}{3}$ cup coconut milk

2 lemongrass stalks, coarsely chopped

2 fresh red chilies, seeded and chopped

3 garlic cloves, finely chopped

1-inch piece of fresh ginger root, chopped

2 tbsp dark brown sugar

2 tbsp chopped fresh cilantro

1 small pineapple, peeled, cored, and finely chopped

3 shallots, chopped

1 tbsp light soy sauce

$\frac{1}{4}$ cup roasted unsalted peanuts, chopped

peanut oil, for brushing

1 Slash each chicken portion diagonally 2–3 times with a sharp knife and place in a shallow, nonmetallic dish. Put 4 tablespoons of the lime juice, the coconut milk, lemongrass, chilies, garlic, ginger, sugar, and cilantro in a blender or food processor and process until smooth. Pour the mixture over the chicken and turn to coat. Cover with plastic wrap and set aside in a cool place to marinate for 2 hours.

2 Combine the pineapple, shallots, soy sauce, peanuts, and the remaining lime juice in a bowl, then cover, and set aside.

3 Brush the electric grill with oil and preheat. Drain the chicken. When the grill is hot add the chicken and cook for 5–7 minutes until cooked through and tender. Test to check that the juices run clear when it is pierced with the point of a knife. If there are any traces of pink, return to the grill for 1–2 minutes. Serve immediately with the pineapple and peanut mixture on the side.

Cook's tip
To make sure that the chicken breast portions are an even thickness, place them between 2 sheets of plastic wrap and pound lightly with a rolling pin or a meat bat.

Variation
This is also a delicious way to cook white fish fillets. Marinate in the mixture for 30 minutes, then grill for 3–5 minutes.

CHICKEN WITH ORANGE JUICE & WHITE WINE

Chicken benefits from a marinade as the flesh stays moister during cooking so it's really tender and full of flavor.

 Serves 4

 Preparation time: 10 minutes, plus 1 hour's marinating

 Cooking time: 5–7 minutes

Ingredients

4 skinless, boneless chicken breast portions

2/3 cup dry white wine

5 tbsp orange juice

1 tsp honey

1 tbsp dark soy sauce

1 tbsp mild mustard

2 garlic cloves, chopped

2 tbsp chopped fresh rosemary

sunflower oil, for brushing

salt and pepper

fresh rosemary sprigs, to garnish

1 Slash each chicken portion diagonally 2–3 times with a sharp knife and place in a shallow, nonmetallic dish. Put the wine, orange juice, honey, soy sauce, mustard, garlic, and rosemary in a blender or food processor and process until thoroughly combined. Pour the mixture over the chicken and turn to coat. Cover with plastic wrap and set aside in a cool place to marinate for 1 hour.

2 Brush the electric grill with oil and preheat. Drain the chicken. When the grill is hot add the chicken and cook for 5–7 minutes until cooked through and tender. Test to check that the juices run clear when it is pierced with the point of a knife. If there are any traces of pink, return to the grill for 1–2 minutes. Season with salt and pepper, garnish with rosemary sprigs, and serve.

Cook's tip
Dark soy sauce is sweeter and less strongly flavored than light soy sauce. It is the type usually used in marinades, while light soy sauce is more of a condiment.

Variation
This is a good way to cook pork tenderloin. Cut into slices 1/2 inch thick and marinate for at least 1 hour.
Grill for 4–6 minutes until the juices run clear when the meat is pierced with the point of a knife.

CHICKEN TANDOORI-STYLE

A tandoor is actually a traditional clay oven but you can still achieve
really tasty results with ready-made tandoori paste and the grill.

○ Serves 4

Preparation time: 10 minutes, plus 2 hours' marinating

Cooking time: 5–7 minutes

Ingredients

4 skinless, boneless chicken breast portions

4 tbsp tandoori masala paste

sunflower oil, for brushing

2 red onions, thinly sliced

5 tbsp chopped fresh cilantro

Garnish

lemon wedges

1 red onion, thinly sliced

1 Slash each chicken portion diagonally 2–3 times with a sharp knife and place in a shallow, nonmetallic dish. Rub the chicken all over with the tandoori paste and let marinate in a cool place for about 2 hours or in the refrigerator overnight.

2 If necessary, bring the chicken back to room temperature. Brush the electric grill with oil and preheat. When the grill is hot add the chicken and the onion slices and cook for 5–7 minutes until the chicken juices run clear when pierced with the point of a knife. If there is any trace of pink, return them to the grill for 1–2 minutes.

3 Transfer the onions to a bowl and mix with the cilantro. Make a bed of the mixture on warm serving plates and top with the chicken portions. Garnish with lemon wedges and slices of red onion and serve immediately.

Cook's tip
If your electric grill isn't big enough to cook the chicken and onions together, cook the chicken first and keep warm while you cook the onions.

Variation
If you want to make your own tandoori paste, combine ⅔ cup plain yogurt, 1 tsp chili powder, 1½ tsp finely chopped fresh ginger root, 2 tsp ground coriander, and 2 tsp ground cumin. Season with salt.

CHICKEN WITH MIDDLE-EASTERN SPICES

Aromatic spices with a slight hint of chili give chicken a really delicious and unusual flavor.

 Serves 6

Preparation time: 10 minutes, plus 2 hours' marinating

Cooking time: 5–7 minutes

Ingredients

6 skinless, boneless chicken breast portions

4 tbsp olive oil, plus extra for brushing

½ tsp ground coriander

¼ tsp ground mace

¼ tsp ground cardamom

¼ tsp chili powder

salt and pepper

couscous, to serve

Garnish

lemon wedges

fresh sage sprigs

1 Cut the chicken into 1-inch cubes and place in a shallow, nonmetallic dish. Combine the oil, coriander, mace, cardamom, and chili powder and season with salt and pepper. Pour the mixture over the chicken and turn to coat. Cover with plastic wrap and set aside in a cool place to marinate for 2 hours.

2 Brush the electric grill with oil and preheat. Drain the chicken and thread onto skewers. When the grill is hot add the chicken and cook for 5–7 minutes. Test to check that the juices run clear when it is pierced. If there are any traces of pink, return the chicken to the grill for 1–2 minutes.

3. Transfer the chicken to warm serving plates, garnish with lemon wedges and sage sprigs, and serve immediately with couscous on the side.

Cook's tip

Always buy spices in small quantities as they quickly lose their aroma and become stale.

Variation

This combination of spices is delicious with lamb. You can use chops or lamb sirloin and grill for the same length of time as the chicken.

HERBED TURKEY SCALLOPS

*Turkey scallops are an economical buy and taste great
marinated in herbs and served with hot fruit.*

Serves 4

Preparation time: 10 minutes, plus overnight marinating

Cooking time: 10 minutes

Ingredients

4 turkey scallops

2 tbsp sunflower oil, plus extra for brushing

6 sage leaves, torn into pieces

½ cup dry white wine

grated rind and juice of 2 limes

4 juniper berries, lightly crushed

4 black peppercorns, lightly crushed

1 tbsp honey

8 slices fresh pineapple

salt and pepper

fresh sage sprigs, to garnish

1 Place the turkey scallops between 2 sheets of plastic wrap and pound lightly with a rolling pin or the flat
side of a meat bat. Transfer to a shallow, nonmetallic dish.

2 Heat the oil in a skillet, add the sage leaves, and stir-fry for 30 seconds. Add the wine, lime rind and
juice, juniper berries, peppercorns, and honey. Stir well and season with salt and pepper.

3 Pour the mixture over the turkey scallops and turn to coat. Cover with plastic wrap and leave in the
refrigerator to marinate overnight.

4 Bring the turkey back to room temperature. Brush the electric grill with oil and preheat. When the grill is
hot add the pineapple slices and cook for 5–7 minutes. Remove and keep warm. Add the turkey scallops
to the grill and cook for 4 minutes. Test to check that the juices run clear when they are pierced with the
point of a knife. If there are any traces of pink, return to the grill for 1–2 minutes.

5 Transfer the turkey to warm plates, top each scallop with 2 slices of pineapple, and garnish with a sprig
of sage. Serve immediately.

Cook's tip
*Crush the juniper berries and peppercorns with a pestle
and mortar or with the back of a spoon.*

Variation
*This is also a good way to cook pork and veal scallops,
which may need a slightly longer grilling time. Try serving
them with grilled apple slices or peach halves.*

TURKEY BURGERS

Low in fat but packed full of flavor, turkey burgers make a delightful change
from their beefy cousins and will be popular with all the family.

 Serves 4

Preparation time: 10 minutes

Cooking time: 5 minutes

Ingredients

12 oz ground turkey breast

4 tbsp fresh whole-wheat bread crumbs

1 small onion, finely chopped

1 eating apple, peeled, cored, and
  finely chopped

grated rind and juice of 1 small lemon

2 tbsp finely chopped fresh parsley

sunflower oil, for brushing

salt and pepper

whole-wheat rolls or Focaccia, to serve

1 Put the turkey, bread crumbs, onion, apple, lemon rind and juice, and parsley into a bowl and mix well
with your hands. Divide the mixture into 4 portions and shape each into a patty no more than 1 inch thick.

2 Brush the electric grill with oil and preheat. When the grill is hot add the burgers and cook, turning
once, for 5 minutes until cooked through. Test to check that the juices run clear when they are pierced with
the point of a knife. If there are any traces of pink, return to the grill for 1–2 minutes.

3 Slit the rolls and add a burger to each. Serve immediately.

Cook's tip
These burgers are slightly more fragile than beef
burgers, so handle them with care when placing
on the electric grill and turning them.

Variation
For a different flavor substitute lime rind and juice
for the lemon, and thyme for the parsley.

CHAPTER 3: FISH AND SHELLFISH

TUNA STEAKS WITH SPICY SALSA

Tuna is an extremely versatile fish—its meaty texture and flavor make it very suitable for cooking on an electric grill.

Serves 4

Preparation time: 15 minutes, plus 30–60 minutes' chilling

Cooking time: 15 minutes

Ingredients

1 tbsp sunflower oil, plus extra for brushing

1 large onion, finely chopped

2 garlic cloves, finely chopped

2 tomatoes, peeled and finely chopped

4 fresh tuna steaks, about 6 oz each

2 tbsp lime juice

salt and pepper

fresh cilantro sprigs, to garnish

Salsa

2 ripe mangoes, peeled, pitted, and diced

2 fresh green chilies, seeded and finely chopped

$\frac{1}{2}$–1 tsp finely chopped fresh ginger root

4 tbsp lime juice

2 tbsp finely chopped fresh cilantro

1 First make the salsa. Combine all the ingredients in a bowl and season to taste with salt and pepper. Cover with plastic wrap and chill in the refrigerator for 30–60 minutes.

2 Brush the electric grill with oil and preheat. Heat the oil in a heavy skillet. Add the onion and garlic and cook over low heat, stirring occasionally, for 5 minutes, or until softened. Add the tomatoes and mix well.

3 Season the tuna steaks with salt and pepper and sprinkle with the lime juice. When the grill is hot add the tuna steaks, then spoon the onion and tomato mixture on top of the fish. Cook for 6–8 minutes until the fish flakes easily with a fork.

4 Transfer the tuna steaks to warm plates and spoon the onion and tomato mixture on top. Garnish with sprigs of cilantro. Stir the salsa and serve it on the side.

Cook's tip

It is very fashionable at the moment to eat tuna steaks just seared on the outside and still rare in the middle. If this is how you like your fish, cook for 3–5 minutes, then remove, and check whether it is done to your liking.

Variation

This salsa also goes well with Lime & Lemongrass Chicken (see page 38).

SWORDFISH STEAKS WITH LIME BUTTER

 Although it's an oily fish, the flesh of swordfish dries out very easily during cooking, so it is always best to marinate it first.

◎ Serves 4

🥣 Preparation time: 15 minutes, plus 30 minutes' marinating

🧤 Cooking time: 6–9 minutes

Ingredients

4 swordfish steaks, about 6 oz each

3 tbsp olive oil, plus extra for brushing

6 tbsp lime juice

1 tsp sweet paprika

generous 1/2 cup sweet butter, cut into pieces

grated rind of 1 lime

1 1/2-inch piece of fresh ginger root, chopped

1 tbsp chopped fresh cilantro

pinch of cayenne pepper

salt and pepper

1 Place the swordfish steaks in a shallow, nonmetallic dish. Combine the olive oil, 2 tablespoons of the lime juice, and the paprika in a pitcher and season with salt and pepper. Pour the mixture over the fish steaks and turn to coat. Cover with plastic wrap and set aside in a cool place to marinate for 30 minutes.

2 Meanwhile, put the remaining lime juice in a blender with the butter, lime rind, ginger, and cilantro. Season with salt and cayenne pepper. Process until thoroughly combined, scraping down the side of the goblet if necessary.

3 Scrape the lime butter onto a piece of foil and roll into a cylinder shape. Chill in the refrigerator until ready to serve.

4 Brush the electric grill with oil and preheat. Drain the swordfish steaks. When the grill is hot add the fish and cook for 6–9 minutes until the flesh is opaque and flakes easily with a fork.

5 Transfer the swordfish steaks to warm plates. Unwrap the lime butter and cut it into slices. Top each fish steak with 1–2 slices of the butter and serve immediately.

Cook's tip

The acid in citrus fruit will start to "cook" raw fish after a while (technically speaking, it denatures the protein). Therefore it is best to marinate for only 30 minutes and for a maximum of 1 hour.

Variation

This is an excellent way to cook any game fish, such as barracuda or shark. You can sometimes find these in the stores; otherwise, make friends with a keen deep-sea fisherman. It also works well with tuna.

SALMON STEAKS WITH PARSLEY PESTO

*With fish, the simplest dishes are often the best and this one
couldn't be quicker or easier, yet it tastes wonderful.*

○ Serves 4
Preparation time: 10 minutes
Cooking time: 7–8 minutes

Ingredients

2 garlic cloves, coarsely chopped
½ cup pine nuts
¾ cup fresh parsley leaves
1 tsp sea salt
⅓ cup freshly grated Parmesan cheese

½–⅔ cup extra virgin olive oil,
   plus extra for brushing
4 salmon steaks, about 6 oz each
lemon wedges, to garnish

1 To make the pesto, put the garlic, pine nuts, parsley, and salt into
a blender and process to a purée. Add the Parmesan and process briefly
again. Then add ½ cup oil and process again. If the consistency is too thick,
add the remaining oil and process again until smooth. Scrape into a bowl
and set aside.

2 Brush the electric grill with oil and preheat. When it is hot add the salmon
steaks and cook for 7–8 minutes until it is opaque and the flesh flakes easily
with a fork.

3 Transfer to warm plates, top with the parsley pesto, and garnish with lemon
wedges. Serve immediately.

Cook's tip

*You can make the parsley pesto with a pestle and mortar.
Put the garlic, pine nuts, parsley, and salt in a mortar and
crush to a paste with a pestle. Work in the Parmesan, then
gradually add the oil until the sauce is thick and creamy.*

Variation

*For a sharper sauce that goes well with the rich flavor
of salmon, replace half the parsley with arugula.*

BLACKENED FISH

Many people think that this popular Cajun recipe is traditional but it was, in fact, created in the 1980s.

 Serves 4

 Preparation time: 15 minutes

 Cooking time: 4–5 minutes

Ingredients

1 tbsp paprika

1 tsp cayenne pepper

1 tsp dried oregano

1 tsp dried thyme

1 tsp garlic powder

oil, for brushing

½ cup sweet butter

4 red snapper fillets

salt and pepper

lime wedges, to garnish

Salsa

225 g/8 oz tomatoes, peeled, seeded, and chopped

3 tbsp finely chopped fresh cilantro

1 fresh red chili, seeded and finely chopped

3 tbsp lime juice

1 First make the salsa. Combine all the ingredients in a bowl and season with salt and pepper. Cover with plastic wrap and set aside for the flavors to mingle.

2 Combine the paprika, cayenne pepper, oregano, thyme, and garlic powder in a bowl and season well with salt and pepper. Brush the electric grill with oil and preheat.

3 Melt the butter in a small pan over low heat. Remove the pan from the heat. Dip the fish fillets into the melted butter and sprinkle them with the spice mix, pressing it on with your fingers.

4 When the grill is hot add the fish fillets and cook for 4–5 minutes until the spice mix is partially blackened and the flesh flakes easily with a fork. Transfer to warm plates and garnish with lime wedges. Serve immediately with the salsa on the side.

Cook's tip
Despite the name, the fish fillets don't turn black all over—just where they come in contact with the ridges of the grill.

Variation
Red snapper is the classic variety for this dish, but almost any firm-textured fish is suitable. You could use sea bass, porgy, and even salmon fillets.

CRAB CAKES WITH SWEET CHILI SAUCE

These tasty morsels are a Thai speciality and can be served as a main course, an appetizer for six, or simply as canapés at a party.

Serves 4

Preparation time: 25 minutes

Cooking time: 15–25 minutes

Ingredients

1 lb cooked crabmeat, thawed if frozen

2 red chilies, seeded and finely chopped

1 garlic clove, finely chopped

1-inch piece fresh ginger root, finely chopped

1 egg yolk, lightly beaten

2 tsp Thai fish sauce

4 tbsp chopped fresh cilantro

$2^2/_3$ cups mashed potatoes, cooled

peanut oil, for brushing

all-purpose flour, for dusting

Sweet chili dipping sauce

6 tbsp sugar

1 cup rice vinegar

2 tbsp Thai fish sauce

4–6 fresh red chilies, seeded and
 finely chopped

1 First make the dipping sauce. Pour 1 cup water into a pan and add the sugar. Bring to a boil, stirring constantly, until the sugar has dissolved. Lower the heat and simmer for 5 minutes, then remove from the heat, and stir in the vinegar, fish sauce, and chilies. Set aside until required.

2 Place the crabmeat in a large bowl and flake with a fork. Add the chilies, garlic, ginger, egg yolk, fish sauce, and cilantro, and mix well. Gradually mix in the mashed potatoes.

3 Brush the electric grill with oil and preheat. Flour your hands, take small pieces of the crab mixture, and shape into balls. Flatten slightly and place on a plate. You should have about 24 cakes.

4 When the grill is hot add the crab cakes, in 2 or 3 batches, and cook for 5–8 minutes. Keep each batch warm while you cook the remainder, brushing the grill with more oil if necessary.

5 Pile the crab cakes onto a warm platter. Pour the dipping sauce into small dishes and serve immediately.

Cook's tip
Thai fish sauce is also known as nam pla and is widely available from supermarkets and Asian food stores. It is made from salted anchovies and used in Thai cooking in much the same way as soy sauce is used in Chinese.

Variation
Substitute 1 lb peeled, cooked shrimp for the crabmeat and serve with dishes of light soy sauce for dipping.

FLOUNDER IN AN AROMATIC MARINADE

As flounder can sometimes be a little insipid, it is a good idea
to boost its flavor with a marinade before cooking.

◎ Serves 4

🥣 Preparation time: 10 minutes, plus 30 minutes' marinating

🧤 Cooking time: 3–4 minutes

Ingredients

2 lb flounder fillets

½ cup dry white wine

½ cup lemon juice

1 tsp light soy sauce

1 tbsp honey

5 tbsp sunflower oil, plus extra for brushing

¼ tsp ground allspice

lemon wedges, to garnish

1 Put the fish in a shallow dish. Combine the white wine, lemon juice, soy sauce, honey, sunflower oil, and allspice in a pitcher. Pour the mixture over the fish and turn to coat. Cover with plastic wrap and set aside in a cool place to marinate for 30 minutes.

2 Brush the electric grill with oil and preheat. Drain the fish. When the grill is hot, add the fish, in batches if necessary, and cook for 3–4 minutes until the flesh flakes easily with a fork. Serve immediately, garnished with lemon wedges.

Cook's tip

Don't marinate the fish for longer than the time specified in the method. The action of the lemon juice in the mixture alters the texture of the fish so that it is partially "cooked" before it is put on the grill.

Variation

You can use any flat fish fillets for this recipe. It would work well with both winter and summer flounder, even lemon sole. Halibut, on the other hand, is not only very expensive but its delicate flavor would be overpowered.

SEAFOOD KABOBS

Skewered food always looks appetizing and is a good way to introduce children to new ingredients and flavors.

 Serves 4

Preparation time: 20 minutes, plus 30 minutes' marinating

Cooking time: 3–4 minutes

Ingredients

12 oz prepared squid sacs	2 red bell peppers
12 raw jumbo shrimp, peeled and deveined	2 fresh red chilies
4 tbsp olive oil, plus extra for brushing	1 tbsp red wine vinegar
1 tbsp lime juice	salt and pepper
3 tbsp chopped fresh oregano	cooked rice, to serve
4 scallions, finely chopped	

1 Open out the squid sacs and score the insides with a sharp knife, then cut into 1-inch squares. Place the squid and shrimp in a shallow dish. Combine the olive oil, lime juice, oregano, and scallions in a pitcher. Pour the mixture over the seafood and toss to coat. Cover with plastic wrap and set aside in a cool place to marinate for 30 minutes.

2 Meanwhile, place the bell peppers on a cookie sheet under a preheated broiler. Broil, turning frequently, for 10 minutes until the skins are charred and blistered. Add the chilies after 5 minutes and cook until they are charred and blistered. Using tongs, transfer the bell peppers and chilies to a plastic bag, seal the top, and let cool.

3 When the bell peppers and chilies are cool enough to handle peel off the skins, halve, and seed. Coarsely chop the flesh and place in a blender or food processor with the vinegar. Process until smooth, then season with salt and pepper.

4 Brush the electric grill with oil and preheat. Drain the seafood. Thread the squid and shrimp alternately onto skewers. When the grill is hot add the kabobs and cook for 3–4 minutes until the prawns have changed color and the squid is opaque. Serve with cooked rice.

Cook's tip
Use wooden or bamboo skewers to avoid scratching the lining of the grill. Soak them in cold water for 30 minutes before using to prevent charring.

Variation
Monkfish fillet works well on seafood kabobs. Cut it into 1-inch cubes and use as well as or instead of the squid.

BASIL-FLAVORED SHRIMP

*This is a terrific dish for informal, if messy, entertaining as it
can be cooked and served in a matter of minutes.*

 Serves 4

Preparation time: 10 minutes

Cooking time: 2 minutes

Ingredients

olive oil, for brushing

24 raw jumbo shrimp

$\frac{2}{3}$ cup sweet butter

24 large fresh basil leaves, torn into pieces

3 garlic cloves, very finely chopped

salt and pepper

1 Brush the electric grill with oil and preheat. Pull
off the heads and peel the shrimp, leaving the tails
intact if you like. Make a slit along their backs and
remove the dark vein with the point of a knife.
Season with salt and pepper.

2 Meanwhile, melt the butter in a small pan over
low heat. Stir in the basil and garlic, then turn off
the heat.

3 When the grill is hot add the shrimp and cook
for 2 minutes, or until they have changed color.
Arrange the shrimp on a serving platter and spoon
the hot herb butter over them. Serve immediately.

Cook's tip
*Be careful not to let the butter brown once it has melted.
Simply stir in the herbs and turn off the heat. If you leave
the pan on the stove, the sauce will remain liquid
and hot as the shrimp take such a short time to cook.*

Variation
*If you're lucky enough to find fresh langoustines, this is
a lovely way to serve them. They will probably require
1 minute more cooking time.*

SEA BASS WITH LEMON SAUCE

There's no doubt that fish and citrus fruits have an affinity, and this delicately flavored lemon sauce complements sea bass perfectly.

 Serves 4

Preparation time: 15 minutes

Cooking time: 20–25 minutes

Ingredients

olive oil, for brushing

¼ cup sweet butter

2 shallots, finely chopped

1 tbsp all-purpose flour

1¼ cups dry white wine

4 tbsp lemon juice

1 lemon, thinly sliced

1 tbsp finely chopped fresh parsley

4 potatoes, scrubbed and very thinly sliced

4 sea bass fillets, 6–8 oz each

salt and pepper

1 Brush the electric grill with oil and preheat. Melt the butter in a pan, add the shallots, and cook, stirring occasionally, for 3 minutes, or until softened. Stir in the flour and cook, stirring constantly, for 1 minute. Remove the pan from the heat and gradually stir in the wine. Return the pan to the heat, bring to a boil, stirring, then lower the heat, and simmer for 5 minutes. Season with salt and pepper, stir in the lemon juice, and add the sliced lemon and parsley.

2 Meanwhile, when the grill is hot add the potato slices and cook for 7–9 minutes until tender. Remove from the grill and keep warm. Brush the grill with more oil if necessary and score the skin side of the sea bass fillets. Add the fish to the grill and cook for 3–5 minutes until the flesh is opaque and flakes easily with a fork.

3 Divide the potato slices among warm plates and add a fish fillet to each. Spoon a little of the lemon sauce over them and serve the rest on the side.

Cook's tip
This is a quicker and easier version of a classic Spanish dish in which whole sea bass is baked on a bed of potatoes.

Variation
Other fish suitable for this recipe include red snapper and porgy. You could also substitute thinly sliced sweet potatoes.

SQUID IN A CITRUS MARINADE

This popular tapas dish can also be served as a main course
with salad or as part of a selection of other tapas dishes.

Serves 4

Preparation time: 15 minutes, plus overnight marinating

Cooking time: 6–10 minutes

Ingredients

1 lb 9 oz prepared squid

1 tbsp olive oil, plus extra for brushing

1 tbsp orange juice

1 tbsp sherry vinegar

¼ cup brown sugar

2 garlic cloves, finely chopped

1 tbsp grated orange rind

1 tsp sweet paprika

chopped fresh flat-leaf parsley and
  lemon wedges, to garnish

1 If you have the squid tentacles, cut into bitesize pieces and place them in a nonmetallic dish. Open out the body sacs and score the insides with a sharp knife, then cut into 2 x 1-inch pieces. Add to the dish.

2 Combine the olive oil, orange juice, vinegar, sugar, garlic, orange rind, and paprika in a pitcher, stirring until well mixed. Pour the mixture over the squid and toss to coat. Cover with plastic wrap and marinate in the refrigerator overnight.

3 Brush the electric grill with oil and preheat. Drain the squid and pour the marinade into a pan. Bring the marinade just to boiling point over low heat. When the grill is hot add the squid, in batches if necessary, and cook, turning the tentacles once, for 3–4 minutes. Keep warm while you cook the remaining squid.

4 Transfer the squid to a warm serving platter and pour over the hot marinade. Garnish with chopped parsley and lemon wedges and serve immediately.

Cook's tip
However you cook squid, you have to keep alert as overcooking will make it tough and rubbery. It's best to check once or twice during cooking to prevent this from happening.

Variation
Scallops also taste delicious when flavored with this marinade. Marinate for 2–3 hours and grill for 4–6 minutes.

Cod Steaks with Caper Sauce

When we think of traditional fish dishes we usually think of parsley sauce,
but caper sauce has a venerable history—and a more interesting flavor.

Serves 4
Preparation time: 10 minutes
Cooking time: 10 minutes

Ingredients

oil, for brushing

4 cod steaks, about 6 oz each

½ lemon

6 tbsp butter

2 tbsp pickled capers, plus
  1 tbsp vinegar from the jar

1 tbsp chopped fresh parsley

salt and pepper

fresh parsley sprigs, to garnish

1 Brush the electric grill with oil and preheat. Season the cod steaks with salt and pepper and squeeze the lemon over them.

2 Put the butter in a pan and melt over low heat. Continue to cook until it turns brown in color, but do not let it become black.

3 When the grill is hot add the cod steaks and cook for 6–8 minutes until the flesh is opaque and flakes easily with a fork.

4 Stir the capers and vinegar into the butter, then stir in the chopped parsley, and remove from the heat. Place the fish on warm serving plates, spoon the caper sauce over it, and serve immediately.

Cook's tip

Capers are the flower buds of a Mediterranean bush.
They are available preserved in salt or pickled in vinegar.
It is the second kind that works best in this recipe.

Variation

For a stronger flavor, stir 1 tablespoon anchovy extract into
the caper sauce just before adding the parsley.

MACKEREL FILLETS WITH HORSERADISH MASH

*Oily fish contain essential omega 3 fatty acids which are important
for good health—what's more, mackerel taste fabulous too.*

Serves 4
Preparation time: 15 minutes
Cooking time: 20 minutes/4–5 minutes' grilling

Ingredients

1 lb 10 oz potatoes, peeled
   and cut into fourths
sunflower oil, for brushing
1 tbsp mixed black and white peppercorns
4 mackerel fillets
½ cup sour cream or
   crème fraîche

4 tbsp milk
1 tbsp creamed horseradish
salt
lime slices, to garnish

1 Place the potatoes in a large pan, add a pinch of salt and cold water to cover, and bring to a boil. Lower the heat and simmer for 20 minutes, or until tender.

2 Toward the end of the cooking time brush the electric grill with oil and preheat. Lightly crush the peppercorns in a mortar with a pestle or with the back of a spoon.

3 When the grill is hot add the fish, sprinkle over the crushed peppercorns, and cook for 4–5 minutes until tender and the flesh flakes easily with a fork.

4 Meanwhile, drain the potatoes well in a colander and return to the pan. Add the cream and mash well with a potato masher or fork. Add the creamed horseradish and stir in well with a wooden spoon.

5 Divide the horseradish mash among warm serving plates and place a mackerel fillet on each. Garnish with slices of lime and serve immediately.

Cook's tip
*Don't bother to skin the fillets before you cook them.
Leaving the skin intact helps to keep the flesh moist and
prevent the fillets from falling apart as you serve them.*

Variation
*This recipe is also good with smoked mackerel.
Buy cold-smoked mackerel fillets (hot-smoked needs
no further cooking) and prepare them in the same way.
Grill for 4–5 minutes.*

CHAPTER 4: VEGETARIAN

Grilled Vegetables with Balsamic Dressing

The sweet, mellow flavor of balsamic vinegar goes
superbly with this colorful mix of vegetables.

 Serves 4
 Preparation time: 10 minutes, plus 5–15 minutes' standing
 Cooking time: 12 minutes

Ingredients

3 tbsp extra virgin olive oil, plus extra
   for brushing
1 red bell pepper, halved and seeded
1 yellow bell pepper, halved and seeded
8 oz young asparagus spears, trimmed

8 oz baby leeks
2 tbsp balsamic vinegar
salt and pepper

1 Brush the electric grill with oil and preheat. Cut each bell pepper half in half again. When the grill is hot add the bell peppers and cook for 8 minutes. Transfer to a dish.

2 Brush the electric grill with more oil, add the asparagus and leeks, and cook for 3–4 minutes. Carefully transfer to the dish.

3 Add the olive oil and the vinegar and season to taste with salt and pepper. Toss gently to avoid breaking up the asparagus and leeks. Transfer to serving plates and let stand until just warm or at room temperature.

Cook's tip
Look for balsamic vinegar labeled "naturale" as this is produced by traditional methods and is aged for at least 15 years. It is very expensive but a little goes a long way and there really is no substitute.

Variation
In the winter, you can substitute salsify for the asparagus. To prepare, scrape the skin of each root and place in water acidulated with a little white wine vinegar to prevent discoloration. Drain, parboil, and then grill.

ASPARAGUS WITH SWEET TOMATO DRESSING

This dish has now become almost as popular as the classic way of serving asparagus with Hollandaise sauce.

Serves 4

Preparation time: 10 minutes

Cooking time: 4–5 minutes/3–4 minutes' grilling

Ingredients

5 tbsp extra virgin olive oil, plus extra
   for brushing

½ cup pine nuts

12 oz tomatoes, peeled, seeded,
   and chopped

2 tbsp balsamic vinegar

1 lb 2 oz young asparagus
   spears, trimmed

1 oz Parmesan cheese,
   thinly shaved

salt and pepper

1 Brush the electric grill with oil and preheat. Dry-fry the pine nuts in a heavy skillet for 30–60 seconds until golden. Tip into a bowl and set aside.

2 Combine the tomatoes, vinegar, and olive oil in a bowl and season with salt and pepper. Set aside.

3 When the grill is hot add the asparagus spears and cook for 3–4 minutes until tender. Carefully transfer to a serving dish. Spoon the dressing over them, sprinkle with the pine nuts and Parmesan shavings, and serve immediately.

Cook's tip
Very young, thin asparagus spears are also known as sprue and are available early in the summer. As the quite short season progresses, the spears become thicker— you can also use these but they may require a slightly longer cooking time.

Variation
If you prefer, you can omit the Parmesan shavings and sprinkle with fresh basil leaves instead.

VEGGIE BURGERS

*Usually vegetarian dishes that copy meat recipes are not very successful,
but these burgers are the exception that proves the rule.*

Serves 4

Preparation time: 15 minutes, plus 1 hour's chilling

Cooking time: 10–13 minutes/5 minutes' grilling

Ingredients

2 tbsp sunflower oil, plus extra for brushing

1²⁄₃ cups finely chopped
  cremini mushrooms

1 onion, finely chopped

1 carrot, finely chopped

1 eating apple, peeled, cored, and
  finely chopped

¼ cup hazelnuts, finely chopped

1 tsp yeast extract

2 tsp chopped fresh thyme leaves

2 cups fresh white bread crumbs

salt and pepper

1 Heat the oil in a heavy skillet. Add the mushrooms and cook over low heat, stirring occasionally, for 5–8 minutes until tender and all the moisture has evaporated. Drain with a slotted spoon and place in a large bowl.

2 Add the onion, carrot, apple, hazelnuts, yeast extract, thyme, and bread crumbs and season with salt and pepper. Mix well with your hands, then divide into 4 portions, and shape each into a neat patty no thicker than 1 inch. Place on a plate, cover with plastic wrap, and chill in the refrigerator for 1 hour to firm up.

3 Brush the electric grill with oil and preheat. When the grill is hot add the burgers and cook, turning once, for 5–6 minutes until cooked through. Serve immediately.

Cook's tip
If you dust your hands with flour before shaping the burgers, you will find the mixture easier to handle and less likely to stick to them.

Variation
For a spicier burger, season the mixture with salt and a pinch of cayenne pepper.

RED, GREEN & YELLOW KABOBS

These colorful skewers may be served as a vegetarian main dish
with rice or as an unusual accompaniment to chicken.

Serves 4

Preparation time: 10 minutes

Cooking time: 6–9 minutes

Ingredients

8 oz green zucchini, sliced

8 oz yellow zucchini, sliced

1 tbsp lemon juice

sunflower oil, for brushing

4 red cherry tomatoes

4 yellow cherry tomatoes

1 red onion, cut into 8 wedges

salt and pepper

cooked rice, to serve

1 Blanch the zucchini slices in boiling water for
1 minute, then drain, and refresh under cold water.
Sprinkle with the lemon juice and season well
with pepper.

2 Brush the electric grill with oil and preheat.
Thread the zucchini slices, cherry tomatoes, and
onion wedges onto wooden or bamboo skewers.

3 When the grill is hot add the kabobs and cook,
turning once, for 5–8 minutes. Divide the rice
among warm plates, top with the kabobs, and
season with salt. Serve immediately.

Cook's tip
Before slicing the zucchini, remove strips of peel along
their length to create an attractive scalloped edge.

Variation
Cut 8 oz firm tofu into cubes and thread onto the skewers
with vegetables. Take care when turning them as
tofu is quite fragile.

GRILLED CHEESE WITH BELL PEPPER SALAD

This cheese acquires a delicious flavour when grilled but
you must eat it immediately to enjoy it at its best.

Serves 4

Preparation time: 15 minutes, plus cooling

Cooking time: 22 minutes/1–2 minutes' grilling

Ingredients

2 red bell peppers, halved and seeded

2 yellow bell peppers, halved and seeded

1 green bell pepper, halved and seeded

1 orange bell pepper, halved and seeded

4 tbsp extra virgin olive oil, plus extra for brushing

$^{3}/_{4}$ cup seedless black grapes

2 tbsp white wine vinegar

12 oz provolone cheese, cut
    into $^{1}/_{2}$-inch slices

salt and pepper

1 Preheat the oven to 400°F. Place the bell pepper halves, skin side uppermost, on a cookie sheet. Roast for 20 minutes, or until the skins are blistered and charred. Using tongs, transfer the bell peppers to a plastic bag and seal the top. Let cool.

2 Brush the electric grill with oil and preheat. Peel the bell peppers and cut the flesh into strips. Place in a bowl, add the grapes, and season with salt and pepper. Add the olive oil and vinegar and toss lightly.

3 When the grill is hot add the slices of cheese, in batches if necessary, and cook for 1–2 minutes until golden brown. Transfer to warm plates and spoon the salad next to them. Serve immediately.

Cook's tip
Cut the flesh of the bell peppers on a plate to catch any juices, then add the juices to the salad with the olive oil and vinegar.

Variation
This treatment also works well for little goat milk cheeses called crottins. You will need 4 of them and they should be sliced in half horizontally.

Vegetable Medley with Tapenade & Walnuts

In Spain they make a version of the famous black olive paste, tapenade, using green olives, which has a slightly sharper flavor.

Serves 4

Preparation time: 20 minutes

Cooking time: 25–30 minutes

Ingredients

olive oil, for brushing

4 slices of crusty bread, such as ciabatta
   or sourdough

1 large eggplant, sliced

2 zucchini, sliced lengthwise

2 red bell peppers, seeded and sliced

2 orange bell peppers, seeded and sliced

8 baby leeks

salt and pepper

Tapenade & Walnuts

3/4 cup green olives, pitted

2 garlic cloves, chopped

1 cup flat-leaf parsley, coarsely chopped

3/4 cup walnut halves, coarsely chopped

1/4 cup pickled walnuts, drained

1/2 cup extra virgin olive oil

1 First make the tapenade. Put the olives, garlic, parsley, and fresh and pickled walnuts in a blender and process until finely chopped. Gradually add the olive oil until the mixture forms a stiff paste. Scrape the tapenade into a bowl, cover with plastic wrap, and set aside until required.

2 Brush the electric grill with oil and preheat. Brush both sides of the slices of bread with olive oil and toast under a broiler until golden on both sides.

3 When the grill is hot add the vegetables in batches and cook as follows: eggplant 8–9 minutes, zucchini and bell peppers 6–8 minutes, and leeks 3–4 minutes, brushing with more oil as necessary. Transfer the vegetables to a dish and keep each batch warm while you cook the remaining batches. Meanwhile, spread the slices of toasted bread with the tapenade and place on warm plates.

4 When all the vegetables are cooked, mix well, then divide them among the toasts. Season with a little salt (bearing in mind that the tapenade will be salty) and pepper and serve immediately.

Cook's tip
Layer the eggplant slices with salt in a colander, let them stand in the sink for 30 minutes, then rinse and pat dry with paper towels. This helps to get rid of the eggplant's bitter juices.

Variation
You can substitute sliced tomatoes for the orange bell peppers, cooking them for 3–4 minutes, and patty pan squash for the zucchini, cooking them for 6–8 minutes.

POLENTA WITH TOMATOES & GARLIC SAUCE

Look for quick-cook polenta as the traditional cornmeal takes a long time to cook—and you have to stir it throughout.

Serves 4

Preparation time: 15 minutes, plus cooling

Cooking time: 10 minutes/5 minutes' grilling

Ingredients

olive oil, for brushing

3 cups vegetable stock or water

1½ cups quick-cook polenta

2 tbsp butter

3 tbsp snipped fresh chives

2 tbsp chopped fresh flat-leaf parsley

4 plum tomatoes, sliced

salt and pepper

Garlic sauce

2 thick slices of French bread, crusts
   removed

3 garlic cloves, chopped

1 cup walnut pieces

3 tbsp lemon juice

7 tbsp olive oil

1 Bring the stock to a boil in a large pan and add 1 teaspoon salt. Add the polenta and cook over medium heat, stirring constantly, for 5 minutes until it starts to come away from the side of the pan.

2 Remove the pan from the heat and beat in the butter, chives, and parsley, and season with pepper. Pour the polenta into a greased dish and spread out evenly. Let cool and set.

3 To make the sauce tear the bread into pieces and place in a bowl. Cover with cold water and soak for 10 minutes. Pound the garlic cloves with ½ teaspoon salt to make a paste. Work in the walnuts. Squeeze out the bread, work it into the paste, then work in the lemon juice. Stir in the olive oil until the sauce is thick and creamy. Transfer to a bowl, cover with plastic wrap, and set aside.

4 Brush the grill with oil and preheat. Cut the set polenta into wedges or rounds. Season the tomatoes with salt and pepper. When the grill is hot add the polenta and tomatoes and cook for 4–5 minutes.

5 Divide the polenta and tomatoes among warm plates and spoon over the sauce. Serve immediately.

Cook's tip

If you want to remove the brown skins from the walnuts, blanch them in boiling water for 1 minute, then drain. When cool enough to handle, rub off the skins with your fingers.

Variation

Substitute ½ cup freshly grated Parmesan cheese for the butter to give the polenta extra flavor.

WARM VEGETABLE SALAD

This colorful medley of Mediterranean vegetables makes a great vegetarian main course or a tasty accompaniment to meat or fish.

Serves 4
Preparation time: 15 minutes
Cooking time: 20–30 minutes

Ingredients

4 tbsp extra virgin olive oil, plus extra for brushing

3 tbsp balsamic vinegar

1 garlic clove, very finely chopped

8 baby eggplant, sliced

2 red bell peppers, halved, seeded, and sliced

4 yellow zucchini, sliced

4 green zucchini, sliced

1 red or white onion, sliced

salt and pepper

1 Brush the electric grill with oil and preheat. Combine the oil, vinegar, and garlic in a pitcher. Season with salt and pepper and set aside.

2 When the grill is hot add the vegetables in batches and cook as follows: eggplant for 8–9 minutes, bell peppers and zucchini for 6–8 minutes, onion for 5–6 minutes. As each batch is ready, transfer to a serving bowl and keep warm.

3 When the last batch of vegetables is ready stir the dressing and pour it over them. Toss well and serve warm.

Cook's tip
Try to slice the vegetables for each batch to the same thickness so that they cook evenly.

Variation
Garnish the salad with freshly shaved curls of Parmesan or romano cheese.

CHAPTER 5: SWEET TREATS

FRUIT KABOBS WITH CHOCOLATE SAUCE

This is guaranteed to delight kids of all ages and is an excellent way of increasing their intake of fresh fruit.

Serves 4

Preparation time: 15 minutes

Cooking time: 5–10 minutes/3–5 minutes' grilling

Ingredients

sunflower oil, for brushing

2 nectarines, peeled, halved, and pitted

2 kiwi fruit, peeled and cut into fourths

2 bananas

1 tbsp lemon juice

Chocolate sauce

6 oz bittersweet chocolate, broken
  into pieces

1 tbsp light corn syrup

1 tbsp sweet butter

1 To make the chocolate sauce put the chocolate, syrup, butter, and 3 tablespoons water in a heatproof bowl. Set the bowl over a pan of barely simmering water and let melt, stirring occasionally.

2 Brush the electric grill with oil and preheat. Cut the nectarine halves into chunks about the same size as the kiwi pieces. Peel and slice the bananas. Thread the fruit onto wooden or bamboo skewers and brush with lemon juice.

3 When the grill is hot add the kabobs and cook, turning once, for 3–5 minutes. Transfer to warm plates. By this time, the chocolate sauce should be smooth and glossy. Pour the sauce into a pitcher and serve with the kabobs.

Cook's tip
These kabobs are also good served with Nutty Yogurt (see page 94).

Variation
You can substitute almost any fruit, such as apples, pears, peaches, and pineapples. Try to make sure that the pieces are all about the same size.

GRILLED FRUIT WITH PAPAYA SAUCE

The fragrant sweetness of papaya and the warm spiciness of ginger turn simply grilled fruit into a special treat.

Serves 4

Preparation time: 15 minutes

Cooking time: 5–7 minutes

Ingredients

1 papaya, peeled, halved, and seeded

¾ cup white grape juice

sunflower oil, for brushing

2 peaches, peeled, halved, and pitted

1 mango, peeled, pitted, and sliced

½ pineapple, peeled, cored, and cut into rings

2–3 pieces preserved ginger, cut into thin batons, plus 1–2 tbsp syrup from the jar

1 Put the papaya and grape juice into a blender or food processor and process to a purée. Press the purée through a nylon strainer into a bowl. Cover and set aside.

2 Brush the electric grill with oil and preheat. If the peach halves are thicker than 1 inch, then slice them in half again.

3 When the grill is hot add the peaches, mango, and pineapple and cook for 5–7 minutes. Check during cooking as some pieces of fruit may be ready before others.

4 Transfer to serving plates. Brush the fruit with the ginger syrup and decorate with the ginger batons. Spoon the papaya sauce around the fruit and serve.

Cook's tip

Make sure the papaya is ripe. It should be golden yellow. Unripe green papayas are quite sour. It is important to strain the sauce to be sure that no stray seeds remain. They have a very peppery taste and would spoil the dish.

Variation

The papaya sauce also goes well with other tropical fruits and with peaches or nectarines.

COCONUT & KABOBS

Spicy fruit kabobs served with chilled coconut-flavored cream
would make a delicious treat on a summery day.

Serves 4
Preparation time: 10 minutes, plus 30 minutes' standing
Cooking time: 3–5 minutes

Ingredients

3 tbsp dry unsweetened coconut

4 tbsp boiling water

$2/3$ cup heavy cream, whipped

sunflower oil, for brushing

$2/3$ cup orange juice

5 tbsp lime juice

1 tbsp white rum

$1/4$ cup superfine sugar

1 pear

2 bananas

2 slices canned pineapple, drained

8 seedless grapes

8 small pieces of preserved ginger

2 tbsp melted honey

brown sugar, for sprinkling

1 Combine the dry unsweetened coconut and boiling water in a bowl and set aside to steep for 30 minutes. Strain into a clean bowl, pressing down on the contents of the strainer with the back of a spoon to extract as much liquid as possible. Whisk the coconut liquid into the cream, then cover with plastic wrap, and chill in the refrigerator.

2 Brush the electric grill with oil and preheat. Combine the orange juice, lime juice, rum, and superfine sugar in a large bowl. Peel, halve. and core the pear, cut it into 8 chunks, and place in the bowl. Peel the bananas, cut each into 4 chunks, and add to the bowl. Cut each pineapple slice into 4 and add to the bowl with the grapes and ginger, and stir well.

3 Drain the fruits and thread onto wooden or bamboo skewers. When the grill is hot add the kabobs and cook for 3–5 minutes until lightly golden.

4 Transfer the kabobs to plates, brush with honey, and sprinkle with sugar. Spoon the chilled coconut-flavored cream on the side.

Cook's tip
You can use grated fresh coconut to make the coconut liquid but do not use the "milk" found naturally in the coconut shell.

Variation
If you prefer, leave the pear unpeeled and substitute pitted cherries for the grapes to provide extra color.

GRILLED PINEAPPLE WITH NUTTY YOGURT

Quick, easy, looks attractive, and tastes scrumptious—
what better way is there for ending a meal?

Serves 4–6
Preparation time: 10 minutes
Cooking time: 3–5 minutes

Ingredients

1 fresh pineapple
sunflower oil, for brushing
$\frac{2}{3}$ cup strained plain yogurt
1$\frac{1}{4}$ cups hazelnuts, skinned and
  coarsely chopped

1 Cut off the leafy top from the pineapple and discard. Cut the pineapple into slices $\frac{3}{4}$ inch thick. Using a small, sharp knife, cut off the skin from each slice, then, holding the slices on their sides, cut out and discard the "eyes." Stamp out the core with an apple corer or cookie cutter and cut each slice in half.

2 Brush the electric grill with oil and preheat. Combine the yogurt and hazelnuts in a bowl and set aside.

3 When the grill is hot add the pineapple slices and cook for 3–5 minutes until golden. Transfer to warm plates and top with the nutty yogurt.

Cook's tip
To skin hazelnuts spread them out on a cookie sheet and roast in a preheated oven at 1350°F for 7–10 minutes. Tip them onto a clean dish towel, fold it over, and rub them firmly with it. If any skins remain stubborn, return the nuts to the oven for a few minutes.

Variation
Substitute bananas for the pineapple. Peel and halve lengthwise, then grill for 3–4 minutes.

Index

asparagus   73, 74
asparagus with sweet tomato dressing   74

bacon   16
bananas   89, 93
basil-flavored shrimp   61
bell peppers   15, 21, 36, 73, 74, 80, 84
blackened fish   55
burgers, homemade   30

capers   66
cheese quesadillas   22
chicken tandoori style   42
chicken with middle-eastern spices   43
chicken with orange juice & white wine   40
chili pork   36
chiliburgers   31
chilies   18, 22, 35, 36, 38, 50, 55, 56, 60
chocolate   88
coconut & kabobs   92
cod steaks with caper sauce   66
cooking times   10
    chart   10–11
crab cakes with sweet chili sauce   56

desserts
    coconut & kabobs   92
    fruit kabobs with chocolate sauce   88
    grilled fruit with papaya sauce   90
    grilled pineapple with nutty yogurt   94
drip tray   6, 11
drunken lamb   32

eggplant   80, 84

fennel   20
fish & shellfish dishes
    basil-favoured shrimp   61
    blackened fish   55
    cod steaks with caper sauce   66
    crab cakes with sweet chili sauce   56
    flounder in an aromatic marinade   58
    salmon steaks with parsley pesto   54
    sea bass with lemon sauce   62
    seafood kabobs   60
    spicy shrimp   14
    squid in a citrus marinade   64
    swordfish steaks with lime butter   52
    tuna steaks with spicy salsa   50
flounder in an aromatic marinade   58
frankfurters   18

fruit kabobs with chocolate sauce   88

grapes   79, 93
grills
    choosing   8–9
    using   9–11
    care   11
grilled fruit with papaya sauce   90
grilled cheese with bell pepper salad   78
grilled pineapple with nutty yogurt   94
grilled vegetables with balsamic dressing   72

ham steaks with parsley butter   37
herbed turkey scallops   44
hints   10–11
homemade burgers   30
horseradish   69
hot dogs   18

kiwi fruit   89

leeks, baby   73, 80
lime & lemongrass chicken   38
louisiana lamb   34

mackerel fillets with horseradish mash   68
mangoes   50, 90
meat dishes
    chili pork   36
    chiliburgers   31
    drunken lamb   32
    ham steaks with parsley butter   37
    homemade burgers   30
    hot dogs   18
    louisiana lamb   34
    steak béarnaise   26
    steak teriyaki   28
    surprise sizzles   16
mixed vegetable bruschetta   20
mushrooms   76

nectarines   89

papayas   90
peaches   90
pears   93
pineapples   38, 44, 90, 93, 94
polenta with tomatoes & garlic sauce   82
poultry dishes
    chicken tandoori style   42
    chicken with middle-eastern spices   43

chicken with orange juice &
    white wine   40
    herbed turkey scallops   44
    lime & lemongrass chicken   38
    turkey burgers   46

red, green & yellow kabobs   77
red snapper   55

salmon steaks with parsley pesto   54
sausages   16, 18
sausage, bulk   31
sea bass with lemon sauce   62
seafood kabobs   60
spicy shrimp   14
squid   60, 65
squid in a citrus marinade   64
steak
    ground   30, 31
    sirloin   26, 29
steak béarnaise   26
steak teriyaki   28
swordfish steaks with lime butter   52

tapenade   80
thai fish sauce   56
tips   10–11
tomato toasts   19
tuna steaks with spicy salsa   50
turkey   44, 47
turkey burgers   46

vegetable medley with tapenade & walnuts   80
vegetarian dishes
    asparagus with sweet tomato dressing   74
    cheese quesadillas   22
    grilled cheese with bell
      pepper salad   78
    mixed vegetable bruschetta   20
    polenta with tomatoes & garlic sauce   82
    red, green & yellow kabobs   77
    tomato toasts   19
    vegetable medley with tapenade &
      walnuts   80
    veggie burgers   76
    warm vegetable salad   84
veggie burgers   76

walnuts   80, 83
warm vegetable salad   84